Spring of Inspiration

Dr. Jeetendra Adhia M.D.

RUDRA
PUBLICATION
...*publishing positivity*...

25/B, Govt. Society, B/h, Municipal Market.
Off. C.G. Road, Navrangpura, Ahmedabad - 380 009.
Ph. : 079-26447393 • Mobile : 098259 25947
email : rudrapublication1@gmail.com
inforudrapublication@gmail.com
www.rudrapublication.com
Buy online www.clickabooks.com

For Home Delivery : Mobile : +91-99241 43847

Mumbai : M : 98212 95281 • 98692 75439

SPRING OF INSPIRATION

Dr. Jeetendra Adhia M.D.

Copyright @ Adhia International

If you wish to give this book as a gift to many, we offers you special discount with the pasting page of your message.

ISBN : 978-93-80420-02-8

15th Edition - 25 Feberuary, 2016

o Typeset o
Manu Patel

₹ 130/-

: Publisher :
Adhia International
Ahmedabad
www.mindtraininginstittute.net
www.drjeetendraadhia.com

Presented with love to

*Hope this book will help
you in realizing the
tremendous
power of your mind.
I am sure you will be
much happier, prosperous
and successful
when you start utilizing
the unlimited power of your mind.*

With best wishes from

Blessings from Saint

Dear Dr. Jeetendra Adhia

Jai Swaminarayan!

You are constantly thinking about the enlightenment of society, especially utilizing the dormant powers of the youth and the development of their personalities. Your lectures, seminars and workshops towards this end are very beneficial to society.

I wish you the strength, confidence and good luck for progressing in this direction.

Pramukh Swami Maharaj
Swami Shri Narayan Swarupdas

This book is dedicated to

my father,

Late Mr. Haridas Devchand Adhia,

and

my mother,

Late Mrs. Shantaben Haridas Adhia

for inspiring me to become

the person I am.

About the book

This book is a translation of my maiden best seller book in Gujarati 'Prerna Nu Jharnu'.

People often ask me, "You are a medical doctor. What inspired you to shift your focus from the human body to the human mind?" Well, the answer is, over a period of time, I came to realize that the mind and the body are very closely related. I have personally witnessed an incident in my family in which the mind-body connection worked a life-saving miracle. I have mentioned it in this book.

Like my original book in Gujarati, this English version also has been exceedingly well-received both in India and abroad. This book has already been translated into Hindi, Telugu, Punjabi and Marathi.

I have a great pleasure in presenting this fifth edtion of 'Spring of Inspiration'. I will be glad to receive your feedback.

Dr. Jeetendra Adhia
Date : 1st June, 2007

The author....

When most people turn 40, they think of slowing down; but not Jeet Adhia. At that age, he decided to go for a career change – from an unnoticed college professor to become a world renowned mind and memory trainer as well as motivational speaker. Since 1995, he has risen to fame with his 'Spring of Inspiration' lectures, seminars and workshops, which he has been delivering at numerous places all over the world.

Popular and recognized as a 'Human Trainer' and 'Developer of Human Potential,' Dr. Adhia also conducts seminars and workshops on a wide variety of topics like Mind Power, Memory, Science of Living, Leadership, Happy Married Life, Relationship Building and Public Speaking – to name a few.

Born in 1951 in Rajkot – Gujarat, Dr. Adhia grew up in a one room house occupied by his parents, grand mother and five siblings. It was this poverty that became his driving force. At an early age, his father had instilled in him the goal of becoming a doctor. Even though it was a far cry from what his environment would allow, he realized this dream when he obtained the MBBS (Bachelor of Medicine, Bachelor of Surgery) degree in 1974. He then went to Mumbai to complete his MD (Doctor of Medicine) in Community Medicine.

In the 32 years of his practice as a Doctor, Dr. Adhia had often witnessed, and had been fascinated by the influence of abstract factors like thoughts and beliefs on the physical body. His reading habit had always reflected this curiosity. Soon he began to see the connection between the mind and body. He was so excited that he decided to make it his life's mission to spread this understanding to others. Thus, the 'Spring of Inspiration' program was born.

Like all growing things, Dr. Adhia's talk series also had a small beginning. Initially, he gave lectures on this topic to small clubs, associations, schools and colleges. But as his reputation as a speaker spread and the relevance of the topic caught on, he began to receive invitations from bigger institutions and corporations.

After great success in India, his fame crossed the national boundary. Over the years he has conducted seminars and workshops on Mind Power, Memory and Relationships in different cities of the world such as London, New York, Hong Kong, Johannesburg, Bangkok, Panyu (China), Chicago, Los Angeles, San Francisco, San Diego, Santa Maria, Raleigh, Dallas etc. His programs are widely covered by print and electronic media in India as well as abroad.

The demand for his lectures had grown so immense by 2003 that he decided to quit his medical college job to devote full time to spread his message. He is now vigorously engaged in actualizing his pet project - the establishment of Mind University. This international institute envisions the participation of scholars and experts from all over the world in the study of and research on the mind.

One frequent longing expressed by many of his 'Spring of Inspiration' audience was to capture the essence of his program in some way and take it home to share it with family and friends and use it for future reference. Dr. Adhia thus came out with the book 'Spring of Inspiration', which was initially written in Gujarati under the title Prerna Nu Jharnu. It has become so popular that it is also available in English, Hindi, Telugu, Punjabi and Marathi. The author has also written many other popular books and produced CDs on various subjects like Mind Power, Memory, Relationships etc.

- **Rupal Shah**

Contents

Of all the discoveries of the last century, the most important one is the discovery of the amazing power of the mind and how to use it.

Meet a great person

Would you like to meet someone who can give you health, wealth, happiness, mental peace, love, inspiration, freedom and everything else that you have always desired? I am sure you would. Who do you think that person is? God? Some Saint? An Angel? Magician?

No! None of these.

Well, that person is

You–yes! Your very own self.

Sounds unbelievable, isn't it? All your life you have

been told that you are not in charge of your own destiny – everything depends on some external factor like the position of the planets, circumstances, karma and so on. Even the kind of shampoo you use is influenced by the media. And you start believing it. This is because you don't know yourself and the tremendous power that is within you. By the time you finish reading this book, you will be aware of this tremendous power, so that you can use it to get whatever you positively desire.

You may wonder how I claim to know so much about your potential, even though I have never met you. It is because there is virtually no difference between you and me, or anyone else for that matter. All of us work according to certain cosmic laws, and by becoming aware of these laws, we realize that our potential – whether yours or mine – is the same. This book takes you on a discovery of these cosmic laws.

Let us ponder over a few questions

Why some people are happy, while others remain unhappy? Why are some wealthy, and others poor? Some are healthy, and others sick? Some are very successful in achieving their goals, while others fail in whatever work they do?

The explanation for these differences is in the people themselves. To understand this, it is necessary to know about the mind, its power and its characteristics.

Each human being has tremendous mind power, but untill now, we have been able to use it to a limited extent, only because we have very little knowledge about it.

"Even the most successful people have been using less than 10% of their mind power."

Think how much of your mind power you have used until now. If you want to know how to develop and use your mind power to its fullest extent, read on.

Let us analyze our lives

Why do we work hard?

If you ask yourself this question, you may mainly get these answers:

To succeed

To be happy

To have peace of mind

Is it necessary that all these people who work hard will achieve all these things?

No!

Why not?

Because...

To achieve all these, we must work sharp and smart.

Sharp Work

What is sharp work?

Once upon a time, there lived a strong young man. The only problem with him was that he was unemployed. Once, he was passing through a timber camp, the manager of the camp saw him and offered a job of cutting wood and gave him a new axe.

The young man started his job of wood-cutting with lot of zeal. At the end of the first day he was able to  cut seven huge trees. The second day he started with the same zeal and the same axe. At the end of the day he was able to cut six huge trees. Similarly on third day, with the same zeal and in the same time, he was able to cut five big trees. His performance came down with every passing day.

On the seventh evening the manager of the timber camp was going around supervising the work. The young man was busy wiping his sweat, having failed to cut a single tree since morning. The boss of the timber camp asked, "Young man, how come your performance is deteriorating day by day?" The young man replied, "Sir, I have been working for the same length of time, with the same zeal and with the same axe. I don't know why my performance is going down every day!"

The manager smiled and asked, "Have you taken any time out of your busy schedule to sharpen the axe?". The young man replied, "Sir, I was so busy in my work that I did not do anything of that kind."

The manager of the timber camp looked straight in his eyes and said,

"Please understand.

It is important to work hard but

It is more important to work sharp.

My question to all of you is...

Are you working hard or sharp?

Do you sharpen your axe regularly?

Think, which axe do we use in our daily life?

We use two types of axes:

1. Body   2. Mind

If we cultivate the habit of sharpening these axes regularly then we will be working sharp.

Let us know more about these axes.

Body (Axe)

We use the following powers of our body regularly:

1. Muscle power
2. Body stamina
3. Reflexes

To sharpen this axe (body) we must:

⇨ Eat nutritious food

⇨ Exercise regular

⇨ Take sufficient rest

Mind (Axe)

We use the following powers of our mind regularly:

1. Knowledge
2. Skill
3. Attitude

To sharpen this axe (mind) we must:

⇨ Develop a positive mental attitude.

⇨ Read inspirational books.

⇨ Relax regularly.

⇨ Participate in self-development programs.

Smart Work

Smart work means working in the right direction and adopting the right method. Right direction means working in the direction of our goal. Right method means making optimal use of our mind and muscle powers in a scientific way.

Working in the right direction - Goal

Ask these questions to discover your goal
⇨ What I do want to be in my whole life?
⇨ What I do want to achieve?
⇨ What I do want to do?
⇨ How do I want to Live?

Imagine a situation in which you are watching a football match. But this match is different. There are no goal posts in this game. Will the game be interesting? You will laugh at my question because the answer is obvious. The game becomes dull without the goal posts. In the same way, life becomes dull even meaningless, without a goal. Quite surprisingly, we often play the game of life without a goal and waste our time and energy.

It is said that ....

"A person without a goal is condemned
to work for a person having a goal".

If you do not have a definite goal, all your qualities and skills are of little use. Unfortunately, few of us have a clear goal in life. It was found in a survey conducted by a University that only three percent of the people have a definite goal in life. Thus, it is not surprising that only a few of us are successful.

 Just imagine yourself on the outskirts of Paris and trying to reach the Eiffel Tower with the help of a map. But there is a problem. The map you are carrying is that of London with the title Paris printed on it by mistake.

Now imagine your condition. Even if you work hard, can you reach the Eiffel Tower with the help of this map? No. Even if you have positive mental attitude, can you depend on this map to reach the Eiffel Tower? No. Even if you have strong faith in God can you reach the Eiffel Tower being guided by this map? No again. Why? The map is wrong, that's why.

So, it is very important to have a right map. Similarly, a map of life is necessary because it always guides us towards our goal. It shows us the easiest and the shortest way to reach our goal.

"Even the most successful people
have used less than
10% of their
mind power."

Working with the right method

Working with the right method means to make the optimal use of our powers in a scientific way. To achieve our goal, nature has endowed us with two powers -

1. Muscle power
2. Mind power

By using our muscle power, we can only fulfill our basic needs just as animals do. But if we want to achieve more than that, we need to use more and more of our mind power.

All of us desire success, happiness and peace of mind, which can be achieved only by understanding and systematically using our mind power.

Each one of us has tremendous mind power. We have been able to use it to a limited extent until now, only because we had very little knowledge about it.

Think how much of your mind power you have used until now. If you want to know how to develop your mind power, keep reading further.

Difference between Brain and Mind

Most people do not know the difference between brain and mind. They tend to use the words interchangeably. Actually, these terms refer to two distinct entities.

Brain is a physical entity. It is a part of our body, a physical reality, which can be seen, touched and destroyed. The mind, on the other hand, is a functional entity. It is an energy, a power like electricity, which cannot be seen. It can only be felt and used in whatever way we desire. Information about the brain can be found in many medical textbooks.

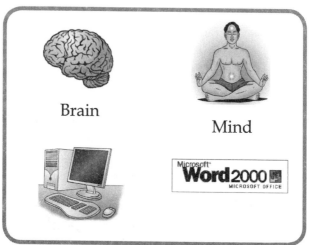

Just remember this in computer jargon; the brain is hardware and the mind, software. In this book, we will concentrate only on the mind.

What is Mind

Mind is energy, a power, very similar to electricity, which cannot be seen or touched but can be used or misused. It is an intangible and invisible power in our body.

We have two types of mind.
- The conscious mind
- The subconscious mind

The conscious mind is active when we are awake. It becomes inactive when we are asleep or unconscious. The subconscious mind is active 24 hours a day. Through the powers of the subconscious mind, we are able to achieve health, wealth and happiness. Until now, we knew very little about it.

Only in recent years, have researchers begun to throw more light on the powers of the subconscious mind.

Functions and powers of the mind

Each mind has different functions and powers.

Conscious mind

1. Sensations
2. Movement
3. Thinking
4. Logic
5. Analysis
6. Interpretation
7. Intelligence Quotient (I.Q.)
8. Identifying and seizing opportunities
9. Judging
10. Decision-making
11. Taking action
12. Making choices
13. Generating desires
14. Serving as a watchman at the gate of the subconscious mind

Subconscious mind

1. Sensations
2. Movement
3. Reflexes
4. Telepathy
5. Radar (Conscience)
6. Memory
7. Emotional Quotient (E.Q.)
8. Treasure of knowledge
9. Wisdom
10. Planning
11. Creating opportunities
12. Mental clock
13. Mental calendar
14. Control over death
15. Control over autonomous nervous system
16. Control over growth
17. Control over immunity
18. Control over healing
19. Control over health
20. Can produce diseases
21. Control over pain
22. Control over every part of the body
23. Influence over the universe
24. Solution of all problems
25. Creative power
26. Personal God
27. Spiritual Quotient (S.Q.)
28. Creative thoughts
29. Spring of inspiration
30. Power generation
31. Magnetic power

Functions and powers of the conscious mind

Let us see the functions and powers of the conscious mind in detail.

1. Sensations

The conscious mind processes the information sent by our five senses: hearing, smell, sight, taste and touch. Since the conscious mind is the 'thinker' and the 'decision-maker,' it makes sense for it to have control over the information obtained from the senses.

2. Movements

The conscious mind controls the voluntary movements of the muscles involved in every action and voice production. That is why, we are able to consciously move our body as we desire.

3. Thinking

When we are awake and conscious, we are continuously thinking. This is a power of the conscious mind. We are free to think either positively or negatively.

Positive Thoughts	Negative Thoughts
• I have a bright future.	• I have a very bleak future.
• People are good.	• Nobody is trustworthy.
• My life is wonderful.	• I have a lot of problems.
• People love me very much.	• People never appreciate me.
• I am very capable.	• I am incapable.
• Good times are ahead.	• Days are very tough.

It is very important to think positively because whatever we think during the working hours percolates into the subconscious mind during our sleep (when the conscious mind is inactive). The subconscious mind takes it as command to work and produce results accordingly (positive or negative).

Even though most people agree that it is desirable to think positive, a lot of people find it difficult to ward off negative thoughts. For them, I suggest one technique – don't worry about controlling negative thoughts. Just make conscious efforts to think positively. The moment you are aware of a negative thought in your mind, just try and replace it with a positive one.

Moreover install positive thoughts on regular basis voluntarily. Do it regularly (without a single day's break) for 21days and your habit of negative thinking will be replaced by positive thinking. Thousands of people have reported that they have used this technique successfully.

In order to help people to become positive thinkers, I have produced a book and compact Disc (CD) on 'Prayer of Mind'.

4. Logic

To use logic means to process information in a systematic way in order to draw correct conclusions. This is done by asking questions such as 'what', 'why', 'where', 'when' and 'how'. We are able to do this only when we are awake. Thus, this power lies in the conscious mind. It is through the power of logic that the conscious mind is able to make choices and take decisions.

5. Analysis

Analysis is a particular type of thinking in which we use logic to see the similarities and differences between various things. Listing advantages and disadvantages is also analysis. We use analysis to assess a situation before taking a decision. The power of analysis is with the conscious mind.

6. Interpretation

After analysis, we make interpretations about a person event or a situation. The power of interpretation is with the conscious mind.

7. Intelligence Quotient (I.Q.)

Intelligence quotient refers to a person's ability to process information and draw conclusions. For example, a student who can solve a math problem very fast is said to have high I.Q. Our school curriculum concentrates on increasing students' I.Q. There is a general belief that people with high I.Q. are destined to be successful and happy in life. This is not necessarily true. What is also needed for a happy and fulfilling life is a high E.Q. (Emotional Quotient) and a high S.Q. (Spiritual Quotient).

8. Identification and seizing of opportunities

There is a saying, "Opportunity does not knock twice." Thus we need to be alert in identifying and seizing opportunities. This is done by the conscious mind.

9. Judging

Judgement is the ability to differentiate between right and wrong. Our conscious mind continuously judges situations and people. We use these judgements to take decisions in our everyday life.

10. Decision-making

After judging we make a decision. To take a decision, we use the powers of thinking, logic, analysis, interpretation and judgment. All these powers are those of the conscious mind.

11. Taking action

After taking a decision, we act on it. We do this either by physical or verbal action. All these are under the control of the conscious mind.

12. Making choices

"To be or not to be?" ponders Hamlet in the famous Shakespearean play 'Hamlet'. We too are confronted with many choices at every step of our life. What career to choose? Whom to marry? What color of socks to wear? Before making these choices, which may range from the really simple to very complex, we use the powers of the conscious mind such as thinking, logic, analysis and interpretation. At times, we might be in a situation where we find it difficult to make a conscious choice. In such cases, the subconscious mind can come to our help if commanded to do so.

13. Generating desires

Think of all the desires you have. Where do they come from ? In the morning when we wake up, desires begin to be generated and stop when we go to sleep at night. So, they originate from the  conscious mind. Desire is the basis of every activity. Therefore, the first and foremost step is to develop a burning desire for achieving your goal.

14. Watchman at the gate of the subconscious mind

This is a very important function of the conscious mind. The subconscious mind has unlimited potential but it has certain shortcomings. I lacks the power of logic and therefore, it cannot differentiate a good command from a bad command.

Thus, in order to prevent mishaps, the conscious mind, which has the power of logic, acts as a watchman at the gate of the subconscious mind, choosing the commands that enter it. If the conscious mind has been trained to allow only  positive thoughts to go through, as in the case of positive-minded people, it will act accordingly.

If the conscious mind has been rendered inactive or has not been trained to filter out the harmful negative thoughts then, negative commands can reach the subconscious mind, leading to undesirable and sometimes catastrophic consequences. Thus, it is very important to train the conscious mind in the identification and elimination of negative thoughts. Positive minded people around you have frequently used this technique with success.

I recall a hospital sign that will interest you.

It has a very powerful message.

HUMANITY HOSPITAL

A person was admitted here. He was bitten by a scorpion. He was treated for 4 hours. He became normal and was discharged from the hospital.

A person was admitted here. He was bitten by a snake. He was treated for 12 hours. He became normal and was discharged from the hospital.

A person was admitted here. He was bitten by a dog. He was treated for 4 days. He became normal and was discharged from the hospital.

A person was admitted here. He was bitten by a man. He is still under treatment and nobody knows when he will be back to normal.

What do you think is the significance of this sign ?

Is it a joke? Or does it have a message ?

Yes, there is a message. If a scorpion, a snake or a dog bites you, you need not worry. Doctor has a solution for it. But if you are bitten by a man then there is no doctor who has a cure for it.

Can a person 'bite' another person?
'Yes' That's possible.

Now you might wonder how?

It is by negative language that a person bites another person.

Let us look at some of the statements that we commonly hear in daily life.
⇨ You are stupid.
⇨ You won't able do this.
⇨ You will never improve.
⇨ What I have done to deserve you ?
⇨ You are the black sheep of our family.
⇨ You will never be able to do anything in life.

Do they sound familier? These sorts of statements bite other human beings. Sentences like these are the root cause of many psychiatric problems like inferiority complex, depression, and many others.

Are you interested in helping society? And more than society, helping your own self? If yes, please follow this simple advice...

Never bite anyone....

... simply because prevention is better than cure.

You may well ask : "what if I stop biting others, but others continue to bite me? How can I protect myself from their bite?"

Your question is valid. Let me tell you how to protect yourself from the damaging effects of negative statements that you encounter in your daily life. It is like protecting yourself from any disease causing agents. We have two ways to protect ourselves :

Vaccine and First-aid

You have probably realized that the human bite is not a physical one but a psychological. Since the process of biting and its effect on us are psychological, the vaccine and first and are also psychological.

Vaccine

The vaccine is a famous sentence created by the famous Viennese Emile Coue.

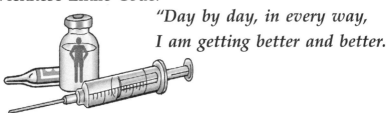

"Day by day, in every way, I am getting better and better.

If you recite this sentence regularly it will protect you against all negative commands. Recite this positive affirmation three times before you start your day.

First-aid

Prervention is always better than
cure. However, that is possible
only if we are in control of the
situation. What if someone,
knowingly or unknowingly,
directs a negative statement at you?

Go for the first-aid now. A stitch in time saves nine.
We know how a neglected wound ends up with more
infection. Use the gatekeeper function of the conscious
mind and prevent these negative commands from
reaching the subconscious mind. It is simple.

Whenever someone hits you (bites you) with a negative
statement, silently say: "Cancel, cancel" and give two
positive commands to yourself.

For example, if someone tells me, "You are stupid,"
instead of arguing with him or getting annoyed, I
say "Cancel, cancel. I am a genius. I am a genius.",
silently to myself.

These two techniques help in preventing negative
statements entering our subconscious mind and save us
from psychological damage. To conclude this chapter,
you have realized the power of the conscious mind.

They may seem numerous, but they account for only ten percent of the mind power. The remaining 90 perscent power is with the subconscious mind.

One big difference between a human being and an animal is the level of development of the conscious mind. Human beings have a fully developed conscious mind while animals have an under-developed conscious mind.

In the case of human beings, the conscious mind gradually develops from birth to adulthood. The subconscious mind is already working at its full potential, right from birth. Yet, most of us know very little about this powerful and larger part of the mind.

Functions and powers of the subconscious mind

Let us take a good look at the functions and powers of the subconscious mind.

1. Sensations

Sensations are experienced both by the conscious and

the subconscious minds. For example, when we sleep at night, our conscious mind is subdued, yet, we are able to the phone ringing or smell something burning. This is because our subconscious mind is always active, and also has the power of sensation.

2. Movement

What happens when you are sleeping and a mosquito bites you? You immediately swat it, even though you are still asleep and your conscious mind is inactive. How does this happen? This is because your subconscious mind, which is active even when you are asleep, has control over your body movements also. Sleep-walking is also an example of the subconscious mind controlling the power of movement. This is an enlightening piece of knowledge. It indicates that bodily performance can be enhanced by giving suggestions to the subconscious mind.

You probably know that Coaches often give a 'pep talk' to the sportspersons before sending them on the track or field. What is that talk? It is just giving positive suggestions.

3. Reflexes

What happens when you accidentally step bare footed on a burning cigarette ? Do you think "Oh, this feels hot. Let me lift my foot." and then you lift your foot? No, you instantaneously lift your foot, and then do all the conscious thinking (and the cursing?). This immediate lifting of the foot is an example of a reflex action which is controlled by the subconscious mind. It protects our body from injury.

4. Telepathy

Has it ever happened to you that precisely when you were thinking of someone, that very person phoned you or called on you? This indicates that when we think of someone with a strong desire or intense feelings, the other person receives that  message and thinks about us too. Our intense feelings attract that person to us. It is called telepathy. Telepathy works no matter how far two people are – even across the globe. This is a power of the subconscious mind.

5. Radar (Conscience)

It is a common experience that whenever we think of doing something wrong, a voice comes from within "Don't do it!" We call it the voice of our conscience. Technically speaking, it is our subconscious mind communicating with our conscious mind. The subconscious mind is the seat of our wisdom, and hence it is in a position to assess the desirability of an action. Thus, it protects us at both the physical and mental levels.

6. Storehouse of memory

Most people believe that memory is a power of the conscious mind, but in reality, it is a power of both the minds. Everyone has immense memory power. The reason why some people seem to have less memory is because they have not cultivated it. Memory is like an wild elephant. It has a lot of power, but you cannot use it if you do not train it.

There are three steps in memorizing:

1. Registration   2. Storage   3. Retrieval

Storage is done in the subconscious mind while registration and retrieval are done by conscious mind. Techniques for training one's memory have been developed by many scientists. I teach people many of these amazing memory techniques which give people a new direction towards success in my Dynamic Memory workshops.

7. Emotional Quotient (E.Q.)

Emotional Quotient is more important than I.Q. Only high I.Q. is no guarantee to success.

There are two types of emotions:

1. Positive emotions   2. Negative emotions

Examples of positive emotions are love, mercy, forgiveness, gratitude, bliss, faith, tolerance and compassion. Examples of negative emotions are fear, anger, hatred, jealousy, sadism, worry, doubt and intolerance.

How do we know that the control over emotions rests with the subconscious mind? Let me explain it this way : We all have heard the saying "Love is blind." Think of how this saying originated. When we are charged with emotions such as love, do we make cool, calculated, logical decisions? In fact, we totally bypass logic in such situations, i.e., we bypass the conscious mind, which could have helped us in making a logical and informed decision. That is why we say "Love is blind."

Similarly, when we are under the influence of negative emotions such as jealousy, hatred, anger, etc., our actions are completely based on negative emotions. After these emotions abate, we usually realize that

41

we have taken an utterly unreasonable decision. This shows that control over emotions rests with the subconscious mind. Otherwise we would have taken logical decisions even under the influence of emotions.

What is E.Q. ?

It is the ratio of positive and negative emotions.

$$E.Q. = \frac{\text{Positive Emotions}}{\text{Negative Emotions}}$$

To increase our E.Q., we must increase the quantity of our positive emotions.

8. Treasure of knowledge

You have possibly heard of Nostradamus and the predictions he made centuries ago. Most of his predictions have come true. A near simialr example is that of Sanjay. He reported every move in the Mahabharata (a Hindu religious epic) war to the blind king Dhrutrashtra while sitting before him in the palace. Both Nostradamus and Sanjay were omniscient-knew everything.

How does this happen? Do we all posses such a power? The answer is yes. The subconscious mind in each of us is omniscient. We all possess a video camera within us which can show or inform us about our past, present and future.

We were ignorant of this fact all these years. Once we understand the power and the working of the subconscious mind and learn how to wield it, we can access its vast storehouse of knowledge. Many experts have developed several techniques of mind control and they teach them in training workshops worldwide. By learning such techniques, we can gain access to the limitless treasure in our own subconscious mind.

9. Wisdom

There is an Hindu saying that "Wisdom is the domain of the old." But in reality, we all have wisdom in the subconscious mind. The ability to take correct decision in any given situation in life is called wisdom. When we are in a difficult situation and cannot come to a right decision, instead of looking elsewhere, we should go within ourselves. Our subconscious mind is always ready to give the wisest counsel. Be sure, wisdom is within all of us, including the young.

10. Planning

If I were to ask you which of the minds is responsible for planning, most likely than not, you would say "Conscious mind." Even I used to believe the same. When my plans failed, I would recall the saying 'Man proposes and God disposes.' I would feel dejected and hopeless and wonder why God is sabotaging my plans. Actually, God was not sabotaging my plans, but my plans were failing because my subconscious mind had other plans for me. This is because the power to plan for our life lies with the subconscious mind. It has made that plan in accordance with the goal we have given to it, and if we consciously make a plan contrary to the subconscious mind's planning, we are destined to fail.

I recall an incident I had witnessed many years ago, but It made sense to me only after I understood this concept. A student whom I knew cleared his school leaving exams and was ranked first in his class. He joined a commerce college with a burning desire to become an IAS (Indian Administrative Service) officer.

During his college years, he thought that he should try to get a part-time job. He applied for the post of a clerk in Life Insurance Corporation of India, but did not clear their selection exam. While he was preparing for the IAS exam, he tried his luck in several career fields. He applied for admission at the Rural Management College and the Xavier Institute of Labor Management. He was unsuccessful in all his efforts. He then read an advertisement for a trainee journalist in 'The Times of India', and applied. He was called for an interview on the basis of his high academic achievement, but was not selected.

In this way a year and a half passed. When it was time for him to take the IAS exam, he passed it in the very first attempt. He was one of the few students from his state (Gujarat) to be selected for IAS. He became the pride and joy of a whole community.

What is the moral of this story? Why was the student, who definitely possessed the caliber of becoming an IAS officer was not selected for positions far below his worth? This is because his subconscious mind had planned for him to become an IAS officer. So any conscious planning that he did, which was contrary to or distracted him from this goal, was disabled by his subconscious mind.

11. Creating opportunities

People often tell me "If I had an opportunity, I would have done ...." I ask them, "Whom do you expect to from an opportunity usually?" They fumble for an answer. Please understand well that we need not wait for an opportunity, but we must create opportunities for ourselves.

Our subconscious mind has the capacity to create opportunities. If we clearly suggest to our subconscious mind what our goal is, it will create opportunities conducive to that goal.

12. Mental clock

At some time or the other, when we planned to wake up early for some important work or event, we set the alarm clock accordingly. But surprisingly, we wake up moments before the alarm was due to ring. How does this happen? The fact is, nature has placed a clock in our subconscious mind – with the alarm facility. This

clock gives us a life-long and maintenance-free service.

13. Mental calendar

Just as our subconscious mind has the facility of an alarm clock, it also has a calendar. With the help of this calendar, the subconscious mind manifests its powers in time. Can you tell me how a baby is born normally 9 months and a week after conception ? This is because our subconscious mind regulates the time of the birth of the infant from a calendar in it. This fact supports the point that nature has provided our subconscious mind with a calendar. Therefore, if we give a specific time limit to our

subconscious mind for the achievement of our goal, it will see to it that we achieve it around the deadline.

14. Control over automous nervous system

There are a number of systems such as the digestive system, respiratory systemm, circulatory system, reproductive system, etc. operating simultaneously in our body. The control over the proper function and coordination of these systems is with the subconscious mind. If any of these systems malfunctions, it results in disease. And when the system regains normal functioning, the body is cured of the disease.

15. Control over growth

Have you ever wondered how a little baby grows into an adult? I am not asking this in the biological sense, but in the cosmic sense. What controls the multiplication of cells? What controls the growth of each and every body part of the baby's body to its normal size and proportion? Can you  consciously grow a large nose instead of a small one? No. This process of growth continues even when you are asleep. This means that the control over body growth is with the subconscious mind.

16. Control over the immune system

An interesting experiment was conducted by researchers at Harvard University (USA). The saliva of a group of students was analyzed to determine the level of antibodies in it. Antibodies are proteins that destroy harmful germs entering the body through food and air.

After the first samples were collected, they were shown a film on the life of Mother Teresa. The level of antibodies was checked again just after they had watched the film. The researchers expected an increase in the antibody level in all the students because they had just witnessed a positive message from the film. They were surprised to get three different results. What they found was that the antibody level had increased in some, decreased in some others and showed no change in the remaining students.

The experiment was continued further. The students were asked to write down their opinion about Mother Teresa and the documentary they had just viewed. The answers were analyzed, and based on the answers the students were classified into three categories. The students who had approved of her activities and praised her were in the positive response category.

The students who had criticized her were placed in the negative response category. The third category consisted of students who gave an ambiguous response.

A clear correlation was found when the outcome of the antibody level tests and the student responses were compared. The antibody level in the students who had responded positively had increased, while the antibody level of the students who had responded negatively had decreased. Those who had not given any specific response found no change in their antibody level.

This proves that a positive mental attitude strengthens the immune system while a negative mental attitude makes one vulnerable to diseases by weakening the immune system. The control over immune system is with the subconscious mind. Therefore, if we want to remain healthy, we should develop a positive mental attitude.

17. Control over healing process

The subconscious mind has control over our healing process. This process continues when we are sleeping and even when we are unconscious. Our thoughts, beliefs, words and attitudes affect our healing system. If we want to improve our healing power, we must think and be positive.

18. Control over health

Our subconscious mind influences the state of our health. If we think positively about health and all other aspects of life all the time, we remain healthy. The subconscious mind stimulates the body to produce health promoting chemicals. Similarly, if we think negatively about health, we become ill. So, we must think, feel and act positively at all times.

19. Can produce disease

I know a lady who had a severe phobia of cancer. Day in and day out, the only thoughts that occupied her mind were those of cancer. She even had many nightmares about cancer. Her heartbeats would race on hearing about someone's death due to cancer. She always feared of being afflicted by this disease. She lived under constant fear of getting blood cancer. As said earlier, fear is a negative emotion. A negative emotion sends negative suggestions to the subconscious mind, and you can now guess what happened after that.

This lady developed a very terrible and rare disease. Our blood consists of three types of cells: white blood cells, red blood cells and platelets. The production and level of these cells in the blood is controlled by the autonomous nervous system. When the white blood cell count of the body increases without any obvious reason, it is known as blood cancer (leukemia).

In the case of this lady, all the three types of cells started multiplying uncontrollably. Even well-known cancer specialists of Mumbai admitted that there was no cure available for her condition and that she would not survive for more than a few months. But she was determined to survive. Since medicine did not have any treatment for her condition, she decided to deal with it by simply using the power of her subconscious mind. This was a real incident which occurred in 1995. At present she is perfectly healthy and all her blood cell counts have returned to normal. The doctors who had diagnosed her disease are surprised to see this 'miracle.'

This incident took place before me and inspired me to conduct extensive study on the powers of the mind. I read a lot of books on the subject which, in spite of my medical training with its emphasis on medicines and surgical interventions, convinced me that mind power can be used far more effectively in healing.

20. Control over pain

You may have heard that some doctors have performed surgery and painless deliveries without the use of anesthesia. How does this work? The doctor gives constant suggestions to the conscious mind of the patient, which are passed to the subconscious mind to block the sensations of pain. The subconscious mind responds to these suggestions. As a result, the patient does not feel pain. We can thus conclude that the control over pain is with the subconscious mind. In our Spring of Inspiration Practical Workshops we teach how to gain control over pain with the help of the subconscious mind.

21. Control over every part of our body

Maharshi Mahesh Yogi is internationally well known for his teaching of Transcendental Meditation. He is also Dr. Deepak Chopra's guru. He claims that

he can levitate his body several inches from the ground during meditation. This is known as Yogic Flying. It makes the body so light that it is beyond the gravitational pull. It is like a gas balloon. This power lies within the domain of the subconscious mind. It shows that by conditioning the subconscious mind, we can gain control over every part of our body.

22. Control over death

When I first began telling people that they have control over their own death (and by that, I do not mean suicide), they were skeptical. But think about it - what is death? Death is the state of the body where all its life support systems have stopped working. We learnt earlier that the control over all our body systems rests with the subconscious mind. When the subconscious mind signals the autonomous nervous system to shut down, death occurs.

I have witnessed this power of subconscious mind in the death of my parents. A month prior to her death in 1995, my mother had started telling everyone that she may not live much longer. All her life, she had prayed for a natural and peaceful death. She also wished to pass away in the presence of her husband. For the fifteen days preceding her death, my father was out of town. She passed away on his return after he had stayed with her for a full day. She was writing the name of God, and without a murmur, her heart stopped working. No disease, discomfort, no pain, just the easing of the soul out of the body.

I did not think much about the significance of the circumstances preceding her death, but when I learnt about the subconscious mind, I was able to appreciate the role her auto-suggestions had played in making her death so peaceful.

Similarly, in case of my father, the subconscious mind also demonstrated its power, but unfortunately, in the opposite way. My father believed that it is a noble duty for every son to serve his parents. He was very keen that his children serve him in his old age and expressed this wish every now and then.

Tell me, when does a son need to serve his parents? The usual answer is-when the parent is weak and feeble or in a diseased state. Since my father had imagined all his life about being served by his children, his subconscious mind provided such an opportunity. In the final five years of his life, he suffered from prostate cancer, which required a lot of home nursing. His state demanded assistance in everything from eating to going to the bathroom. All of us, my brother and sisters came to my home and, served him one by one. Thus, his heartfelt wish was fulfilled. But he had to suffer a lot of pain; pain which could otherwise have been avoided, had he programmed his subconscious mind appropriately.

It is worth thinking about how many such self-damaging beliefs we hold that could lead to self-destructive situations. Dr. Deepak Chopra's immortal book Ageless Body, Timeless Mind, explains in great detail, going down to the atomic level, how thoughts and intentions influence our ageing process and death.

23. Influence over the universe

Our subconscious mind has influence not only over ourselves, but also over the entire universe. This may seem quite an overstatement to you. But let me explain. It is said that Moses parted the waters of the Red Sea to

lead the Israelites to the Promised Land. This has been so beautifully portrayed in the film "The Ten Commandments,

Here is another example. What happens when we a drop stone in water? According to common observation, it sinks. Yet, in the Hindu epic Ramayana, when the monkey devotees of Lord Rama carried and dropped stones in the sea with 'Rama' written on them, they floated. Not only did they remain afloat, they also formed a bridge from India to Sri Lanka! What was happening here? I believe that the devotion that the monkeys had towards Rama activated their subconscious mind so strongly that they even made stones float.

Here's another example of a legendary saint Narsinha Mehta from Junagadh in Gujarat (India). Two episodes from his life are very illustrating. First is the marriage of his daughter Kunwarbai. Her marriage was celebrated with pomp and gaiety even though Narsinha Mehta was penniless. It is believed that God himself had supplied the resources for the ceremony. In the second incident, Narsinha Mehta's Promissory Note was accepted by his banker even though he had no bank account This illustrates that our subconscious mind can call upon anyone, even the Supreme power, for help, whenever needed.

You have probably heard of the unbelievable powers of the two Indian Ragas: Raga Deepak and Raga Malhar. (The raga is a systematic classification of the song. Deepak is a lamp with an open flame while Malhar is rain). History provides evidence that when

 Tansen sang the Deepak Raga, the heat generated in the atmosphere was so much that the surroundings had caught fire. Thereafter, the two sisters. Tana and Riri had extinguished the fire by calling upon the rains to pour by singing Raga Malhar. In this way, the subconscious mind can influence anything in the Universe. There are numerous examples of the universe supporting pure personal intentions.

24. Solution to all problems

When we are stumped by a problem, be it financial, health-related or social, we often try to solve it by consciously thinking about it and looking for a solution. We usually do one or more of the following things:

1 Approach a family member or a friend or any knowledgeable or wise person for advice.

2 Go to a psychic or an astrologer, who attempts to find a solution from the cosmic power.

3 Approach the Supreme power through prayers.

These are some of the good resources to solve our problems. However, there is a powerful resource at your disposal any time you wish to access it.

The subconscious mind had a fascinating role in the discovery of Insulin. Before the discovery of Insulin, there was no medicine available to control diabetes. Dr. Fredrick Banting, a Canadian physician, was working hard on a solution to this problem. One night he had a dream in which the exact steps that would make his formula work. The very next day, he tried out the solution suggested in his dream, and it worked! That's how Insulin was discovered! The same method was repeated in the invention of the sewing machine by Elias Howe. Churchill is said to have thought out his war strategies with the aid of his subconscious mind. Similarly, we can give our subconscious mind a try.

Next time this happens to you, just approach your subconscious mind. Relax and attain the Alpha state of mind (more on this later) and tell your subconscious mind about your problem. It will communicate a solution to you. I feel this is the best option because the subconscious mind is a storehouse of wisdom and knowledge and has the power to solve your problems. Why not tap it to solve your own problems? It will seldom disappoint us.

25. Creative power

All the wonderful creations in the world – the Taj

Mahal, the Eiffel Tower, the Microsoft Corporation etc. are creations of someone's subconscious mind. All of us have this power and that is why I suggest that you create something before you leave this planet. The creation may not be only a physical monument, but a legacy of positive and useful creation. It could be a song, a dance, a book, or a life changing thought, prophesy or...

26. Personal God

The Almighty has given us the subconscious mind as his agent to help us. To feel the presence of the Almighty, all we have to do is go within ourselves. Every major religion says that the Almighty is in you. Our subconscious mind is a part of the Infinite Intelligence. But we were unaware about it and therefore never approached it. Once we become aware, we will feel the power and presence of the Almighty within us.

All of us have a subconscious mind that listens to our problems, gives solutions, provides us with unending opportunities, health, wealth, peace and the strength to draw the cosmic power to fulfill all our desires. If we utilize its power for the betterment of humankind, the world will surely become a beautiful place to live in.

27. Spiritual quotient (S.Q.)

What is spirituality?

I believe that maintaining harmony or congruency between thinking, speaking and doing is spirituality. Let us look at some examples of high and low S.Q.

High S.Q.	Low S.Q.
⇨ To do a job honestly.	⇨ To take bribe.
⇨ To repay a loan in time.	⇨ To default repayment of a loan.
⇨ To maintain values in business.	⇨ To be immoral.
⇨ To keep promises.	⇨ Illegal occupation of rented property.

The role and significance of S.Q. is far greater than I.Q. and E.Q. for remaining happy in life. Well-known personalities like Swami Vivekananda, Mahatma Gandhi, Mother Teresa, Ramkrishna Paramhansa, Martin Luther King Jr. etc., all had an exceptionally high S.Q. That is why they are considered as saints. Today, people are concerned only with the development of I.Q. They overlook the importance of E.Q. and S.Q. and therefore, live miserably.

28. Creative thoughts

The subconscious mind is the origin of creative thoughts or new ideas. We can create whatever we want, with its help. That creation can be a movie, a novel, an industry or any small or big innovative thing.

29. Spring of inspiration

Many people ask why I have titled this book as 'Spring of Inspiration' instead of 'Mind Power.' My reply is that our subconscious mind is the real source of inspiration. My subconscious mind inspired and helped me to write it.

Usually people seek inspiration from outside. But, they do not know that there is a continuous stream of inspiration flowing within them. Whenever we decide to work for the achievement of a mighty goal, our subconscious mind provides us with the required inspiration. This inspiration is very important in the achievement of every goal because it motivates us towards its completion. The very fact that you were tempted to read this book shows that you were inspired from within. This book will help you access that spring of inspiration further as it does for me.

30. Power generation

Many people feel that they are past the age when they can set a goal and accomplish it. But remember, once we decide upon a goal and pass it to our subconscious mind, it generates the needed energy within us to realize the goal. The flow of energy continues till we accomplish the goal.

For example, in Hindu society, when parents decide to get their child, whether son or daughter married, a

new and strong flow of energy is seen in them. You

see them more active during the event than during their heyday. From where does this energy come? It came from the generator of the subconscious mind.

31. Magnetic power

There is a very touching story in the Ramayana (a Hindu epic) about a tribal woman named 'Shabri' who had an intense desire for Lord Rama to come and visit her house. If you think about it, it seems to be a very far-fetched desire. Why would Lord Rama visit the house of an unknown tribal woman? But as we all know, it happened. On his way to search Sita (his kidnapped wife), Rama stopped at the house of Shabri. Without having the knowledge of the subconscious mind, how would one explain this incident? Shabri's burning desire activated her subconscious mind which made Rama visit her place. In a way, Shabri's subconscious mind created a 'magnetic' force which attracted Rama to her house. Similarly our subconscious mind can create a magnetic force to attract anything we desire. It could be health, wealth, love, relationships, mental peace and the list is endless. If we realize and use this, our life would be much different.

How to develop mind power

Nature has given us these powers with one condition.

$$\boxed{\textbf{Use it or lose it.}}$$

It means that if you don't use a body part that has been given to you, it will slowly atrophy and you will not be able to use it in future.

How do we develop our body power.

We develop our body by giving it proper nutrition and by doing physical exercise regularly.

In the same way, we can develop our mind power by

- giving proper nutrition in the form of positive thinking, positive speaking, positive reading, etc. and

- doing regular exercises of the mind in the form of relaxation, meditation, visualization, etc.

Different names of the mind

There are many different names of the conscious and subconscious minds which you may find at different places in different books.

These names are as follows:

Conscious mind	Subconscious mind
• Logical mind	• Illogical mind
• Analytical mind	• Creative mind
• Left brain	• Right brain
• Outer mind	• Inner mind
• Known mind	• Unknown mind

Whenever you come across such names correlate them with the conscious or the subconscious mind as appropriate.

ICEBERG

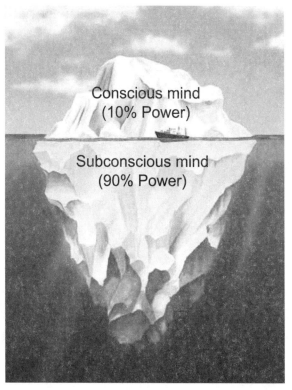

We all know that an Iceberg is a huge chunk of ice floating in the ocean. The known fact about an iceberg is that only 10 percent of it remains above the surface of the water, the remaining 90 percent lies submerged in water, out of sight.

Our mind has a similar characteristic. The mind having only ten percent power, i.e., the conscious mind, is obviously known, while the mind possessing 90 percent power, i.e., the subconscious mind, lies hidden inside us.

Characteristics of the mind

Before we proceed to understand how to use our mind power, let, us first take a look at the different characteristics of both the minds.

The following are the different characteristics of these minds:

Conscious mind	Subconscious mind
1. 10 percent power	1. 90 percent power
2. Human powers	2. Divine powers
3. Works when we are awake	3. Works 24 hours
4. Master	4. Subordinate
5. Executes	5. Plans
6. Analyzes	6. Creates
7. Has limitation of place and time	7. Has no limitation of place and time
8. Can be trained	8. Doesn't require training
9. Thinks before actions	9. Cannot think
10. Uses logic	10. Has no logic
11. Understands jokes	11. Doesn't understands jokes
12. Sets goals	12. Achieves goals
13. Has filter	13. No filter
14. Limited powers	14. Unlimited powers
15. Aladdin	15. Genie

Now let us analyze each one of these characteristics in detail.

1. Proportion of power

The conscious mind has only ten percent of the total mind power. The remaining 90 percent is with the subconscious mind. You may have been aware of the power of your conscious mind, and may have used ten percent of that mind power at the most. Yet, you may have been very successful. Now imagine the situation when you begin using 20 percent of your mind power, or 30 percent! even 50 percent!

2. Human powers and Divine powers

Our conscious mind's powers are human powers. All these powers are normally used by all human beings. The powers of the subconscious mind are divine powers. Using the power of the subconscious mind we can create a miracle in our and anyone else's life.

3. Working schedule

Our conscious mind is active only when we are awake. It is inactive when we are sleeping or unconscious. On the other hand, the subconscious mind is active 24 hours a day, right from our birth till our death - without a break or rest..

4. Boss – Subordinate

Make a guess – who is the master and who is the servant between the conscious mind and the subconscious mind? You might feel that the

subconscious mind is the boss, since it possesses 90 percent of the power, while the conscious mind is the subordinate, since it has only 10 percent of the power. Actually, the opposite is true. Even though the subconscious mind is having 90 percent of the power, it is the subordinate, while the conscious mind is the boss, in spite of it possessing a meager 10 percent of the total power. The conscious mind is the boss because it possesses the powers to think, to use logic, to analyze, to judge and then take decisions which are the essential qualities of a boss.

5. Planning – Execution

Planning is done by the conscious mind, while the execution of that plan is done by the subconscious mind.

6. Analytical – Creative

The conscious mind possesses analytical power while the subconscious mind possesses creative power.

7. Limitation of time and space

The conscious mind is limited by the dimensions of time and space. This is not so in the case of the subconscious mind, i.e., the subconscious mind can exert control beyond the dimensions of time and space. For example, it can even influence things miles away from a person. The conscious mind can work only here and now; it cannot go beyond.

8. Requirement of training

Faculties of the conscious mind, such as thinking, logic, analysis, etc., need to be in order to be trained utilized to its maximum potential. The subconscious mind does not need any such training. It is equally effective for all people, irrespective of their age and education.

9. Negative commands

The subconscious mind has the tendency to act faster on negative commands than on positive ones. For example, you tell your child: "You are stupid, you will never improve." Now, the subconscious mind of a child is very susceptible because its logic (a function of the conscious mind) has not yet fully developed. Thus, the  negative command will reach the child's subconscious mind and it will start working on it to make the command a reality. And then you will wonder why your child never improved.

Quite often we also give negative commands to ourselves unknowingly. We utter sentences like "Nobody understands me," "I am not capable of doing anything," "Success always eludes me," "I am going crazy," etc. Even if just one such command reaches our subconscious mind, it can ruin our life.

I believe that 'Bad Luck' is what people bring upon themselves by their habit of negative thinking and auto- suggestion. People who constantly keep on blaming their bad luck for their misery need to understand that if they change their habit of negative thinking to a habit of positive thinking, they can surely change their bad luck into good luck.

10. Logic

Our conscious mind possesses the power of logic, while our subconscious mind does not have such power. It acts as a humble servant and carries out all the orders of the conscious mind without any argument or resistance.

11. Subconscious mind cannot distinguish between a real command and a command given in humor.

Even if jokingly you say self-deprecating sentences like – "What do I know? I am stupid after all.", your subconscious mind will start working on it as if it were a genuine command. So beware of such humor. Humor causes laughter, which is considered good medicine, but it can be poison as well.

12. Goal-setting and goal-achieving

Before we set a goal, we need to think, analyze, interpret and judge. These all are powers of the conscious mind.

Thus, goal-setting is a function of the conscious mind. Once we decide a goal and pass it on to our subconscious mind, it starts planning to make it a reality. It creates opportunities, solves problems and creates favorable environment for our goal, which are to be understood and seized upon by our conscious mind.  Gradually, the goal becomes a reality. This is a sure way of achieving success.

13. Filter

Nature has provided us with a filter that protects our subconscious mind from negative suggestions. This filter is controlled by the conscious mind. If we do not use this filter effectively, negative suggestions will reach our subconscious 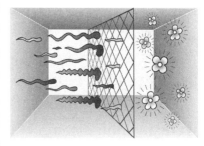 mind uncensored, and the subconscious mind will start acting on them and make our life miserable.

14. Extent of power and knowledge

The conscious mind has limited power and knowledge,

while the power and knowledge possessed by the subconscious mind is unlimited. Therefore, the conscious mind need not direct the subconscious mind in the process of goal-achieving in any way. Our subconscious mind has all the knowledge and power required to convert our goals into reality.

15. Aladdin – Genie

You must have heard the story of Aladdin and his magic lamp. When Aladdin rubbed his magic lamp,

a genie would appear at his service and do whatever Aladdin desired. As a child, I believed this to be only a piece of fiction, but as I grew up, I wondered if it was really possible to get such a magic lamp! I have now discovered that we all have such a lamp within us – our mind. The consious mind and the subconscious mind can also be compared to Aladdin and the genie. Whatever the conscious mind orders, the subconscious mind works to make it a reality.

What we need to know is how to rub this magic lamp so that it does what we want it to do, bring us what we want it to bring, and create what we want it to create.

Network of the subconscious mind

The computer would serve as a good example here. A computer network is formed when many computers are interconnected. Computer network is controlled by one central computer called the 'server.'

A similar relationship exists between all our subconscious minds. The subconscious mind of every human being is interconnected with the subconscious mind of every other person by some form of cosmic network. It is due to this universal network that telepathy becomes possible. The Supreme Power acts as a server for this universal network. The only point that differentiates this particular cosmic network from a computer network is the absence of cables.

A person is declared dead by doctors when his autonomous nervous system shuts down. It means that his subconscious mind has stopped working. According to popular Hindu and other religious beliefs, death is what happens when the soul departs from the body and unites with the Infinite Intelligence (God). If we look at it from this perspective, we can believe that the subconscious mind is our soul itself. Every soul is connected by this universal network.

Every subconscious mind has a large storehouse of memory. This memory can be lost at times, but our network server (the Almighty) with an infinite memory space is said to have a permanent record, which can never be lost under any circumstance. In Hindu religion, this vast memory book is known as the 'Records of Chitragupta.'

Interestingly, the word Chitragupta consists of two concepts. 'Chitra' is picture or that which is visible and "gupta" is that which is hidden, secret, or unknown. It obviously covers both the conscious and subconscious minds.

Location of mind
in the human body

Our conscious mind is located in our brain. According to a yogic belief, our body has six plexuses or "Chakras" (energy centers). One of them, known as the Surya Chakra or the main energy center, is located approximately two to three inches above the navel and behind the stomach.

It is also known as the Solar Plexus. It is a network of interwoven nerves, and it is also the seat of our subconscious mind in our body. This is why subconscious mind is also known as the abdominal brain. The Solar plexus or the subconscious mind is connected to the conscious mind through the Vagus nerve.

Different states of mind

To understand our mind better, we need to go into some technical details. We all are aware of the E.C.G. (Electro Cardio Gram) machine. It measures the electromagnetic waves generated by the heart. E.C.G. is used to record the functioning of the heart.

Just as our heart emits electromagnetic waves, our brain too emits such waves. These waves can be measured and recorded with the help of E.E.G. (Electro-Encephalo- Gram) machine. E.E.G. is useful in recording the functioning of the brain.

Through research it has been found that E.E.G. waves are emitted from a normal human brain and they are classified into four levels or 'states' based on their frequency.

Look at this table carefully.

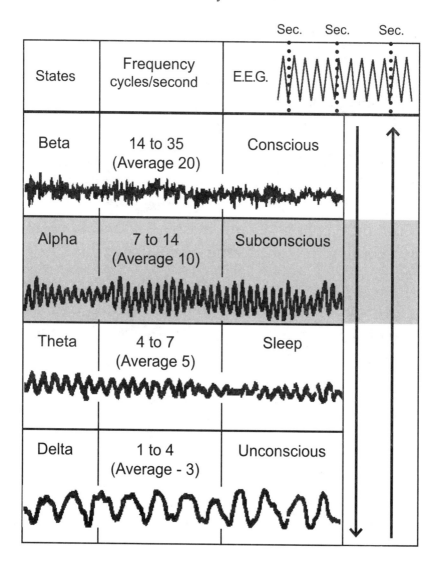

States	Frequency cycles/second	E.E.G.
Beta	14 to 35 (Average 20)	Conscious
Alpha	7 to 14 (Average 10)	Subconscious
Theta	4 to 7 (Average 5)	Sleep
Delta	1 to 4 (Average - 3)	Unconscious

The four states of mind are named after the Greek letters – Beta, Alpha, Theta and Delta.

Beta :   The state of mind when we are completely conscious and awake.

Alpha :   The state of mind when we are not completely conscious or asleep but subconscious. It is a 'meditative' state.

Theta :   The state of mind when we are asleep.

Delta :   The state of mind when we are unconscious.

When the mind is completely alert, i.e., when we are in the Beta state, the frequency of the brain waves is between 14 and 35 cycles per second, the average being 20 cycles per second. When we are in the Alpha state of mind, the frequency varies from seven to 14 cycles per second and we are in the subconscious state of mind. In the Theta state of mind, the frequency of the brain waves is between four and seven cycles per second and we are asleep. When we are in the Delta state of mind, the frequency of the brain waves is between one and four cycles per second and we are unconscious. A dead body does not emit any waves, and the frequency is zero.

The Alpha state of mind

When we are in Beta state of mind, i.e., when we are awake (conscious), our conscious mind is highly active and the subconscious mind is inactive. When we are in Theta state of mind, we are asleep. At that time our subconscious mind is highly active and conscious mind is inactive. But between these two states there is Alpha state of mind in which both our conscious and subconscious minds are active and communication becomes possible between them. So the Alpha state is most important among these four states of mind.

In this state, our subconscious mind is receptive to messages from our conscious mind. Therefore, it is essential for us to learn to attain the Alpha state of mind so that we can effectively give commands to our subconscious mind. If we give commands to our subconscious mind while in the. Beta state, our logic will resist the commands and prevent them from reaching the subconscious mind effectively. This is because during the Beta state, the mind is more logical and analytical. Therefore, the Alpha state, in which the conscious mind is subdued, proves to be the most effective state to send suggestions to our subconscious mind.

Scientific research shows us how the Alpha state of mind can be achieved. It can be achieved in two ways: One is through the natural process and the other is through the use of mind control methods. We pass through the Alpha state naturally just before we fall asleep and just before we are fully awake in the morning. We can also achieve this state through mind control methods. These can be learned very easily and used whenever we wish to go into the Alpha state.

One such method is Relaxation, which is very easy to learn and practice.

We have produced a Compact Disc (CD) on Relaxation. You may use this CD to reach Alpha state easily.

Relaxation

7 to 14 cycles / sec.

Electromagnetic waves

Relaxation is a technique for reaching the Alpha state of mind. This is done by focusing on various parts of our body and relaxing them one by one by giving suggestions or by focusing on the process of breathing. When the body relaxes, the mind automatically relaxes, and this further relaxes the body. It is like a mutually beneficial cycle.

When we consciously concentrate on the breathing process or on relaxing our physical body, the brain frequency starts declining and comes down to the Alpha level, i.e., between 7 and 14. It is a divine experience. After we come out of this state, we feel very relaxed and refreshed. Just 20 minutes of relaxation gives us the benefits of two hours of natural sleep. In the beginning, you may need someone to give you repeated suggestions for relaxing. These suggestions can be recorded on an audio device and you can play it for relaxing. Daily practice of Relaxation, at a fixed time and place, brings wonderful results.

How can we use our subconscious mind?

As mentioned earlier, our subconscious mind is very similar to a computer. We need a specific program to get our subconscious mind to function as per our requirements. This program can be of two types: ready-made or self-made.

(A) Ready-made programs

Characteristics of a ready-made program:

⇨ Expensive

⇨ Quality may not be reliable

(B) Self-made programs

Characteristics of self-made programs:

⇨ Free

⇨ Quality more reliable

What is a ready-made program? An example of a ready-made program is a forecast made by an astrologer about our future. This type of program has two main drawbacks: first, we need to incur some cost and second, the quality may be questionable. Also, our computer (subconscious mind) might get infected by some corrupt programs. Let me illustrate this with the help of an example.

Once, a man who strongly believed in astrology approached an astrologer in whom he had deep faith

The astrologer said that he was destined to die at the end of one month. The man believed in his forecast, and started thinking, talking and behaving as if he was really going to die at the end of the month. He could vividly see his impending death. He readily accepted the forecast as an inevitable fate. And as predicted, he died at the end of the month. This is an illustration of a ready-made program. If the man had rejected the forecast as superstition, he would not have died. This could have been done if he had consciously used his logical power and filtered out the negative program. Thus, the factors responsible for his death were his inability to block the negative suggestions from reaching his subconscious mind and his unshakable faith in the astrologer.

As you know, control over death is a power of the subconscious mind. So what do you find more acceptable – a ready-made program or a self-made one? Obviously, the better choice is a self-made program, which is free of cost and most reliable.

Conscious mind visualizes
Subconscious mind actualizes

How to do our own programming

To enjoy happiness and unending success in life, it is essential to follow these steps for self-programming. There are eight steps in all and each one of them is important.

Step 1: Commit yourself to a mighty thought.

Step 2: Make a map of your life.

Step 3: Develop a strong belief conducive to your goal.

Step 4: Charge your goals with positive emotions.

Step 5: Visualize your goal under relaxation daily.

Step 6: Give auto-suggestions.

Step 7: Use maximum catalysts.

Step 8: Wait patiently for the results.

Let us elaborate on each of these steps.

1. Commit yourself to a mighty thought

Now that you are becoming aware of the potential of your mind, why not use it for a worthy cause. Commit yourself to the upliftment of your own self, family, society and the entire human race. Such a commitment will provide you with a worthy goal.

2. Make a map of your life

You need to give a definite form to your goal. Your goal should be personal, positive, practical, time-bound, measurable and to some extent, flexible. Such a well-decided goal will inspire you to work in the right direction.

You will also experience real joy and enthusiasm. I have come across many people who do not have a goal of their own and so they work towards the goals of others. They are not really happy. I am sure you do not wish to be like them. A goal is your commitment for the fulfillment of a specific purpose. You should decide a worthy goal that interests you and it will give you a sense of purpose in your life.

3. Develop a strong belief conducive to your goal

Whatever our subconscious mind accepts to be true becomes our belief. If our beliefs are conducive to our goal, they will help us in the process of achieving it. If they are contrary to our goal, they will prevent us from achieving our goal. For example, Mr. Leader decides upon the goal to become a successful politician. But his belief is that politics is a dirty business and no politicians are honest. For this reason, he will never succeed in achieving his goal, for the goal is completely contrary to his belief. In short, only when our beliefs are conducive to our goal, we can achieve it.

Do you know what is written in the dictionary of God? There is only one word written  repeatedly millions of times, "Tathastu". It means "So be it" (granted). So whatever we think, believe and say or whatever we pray. God only says "Tathastu". For example, if you say, "I am successful", God says, "Tathastu" or if you say "I am a failure.", God says, "Tathastu". So you have to decide on what you want "Tathastu" (So be it).

4. Charge your goals with positive emotions

Our goal should be such that whenever we think of it, we should get charged with positive emotions. Our heart should start pounding and our adrenaline secretion should go up. This hormone has a deep impact on the subconscious mind. It strengthens the image of our goal and makes it clear enough for the subconscious mind to convert it into a reality. For example, if Mr. Flight intends to become a pilot, the mere sight of a plane flying in the sky should excite him. If Mr. Romeo intends to meet a specific person, the mere thought or picture of that person should increase the adrenaline level in his blood. This usually happens in the case of young lovers. We should have similar excitement for all our goals. Only then, can we achieve them easily and quickly.

You may wonder how you can know if the adrenaline level in your body has increased. Usually, when the adrenaline level in the body increases, blood circulation in the body speeds up, heart beats increase and the respiration rate goes up.

5. Visualize your goal under relaxation daily

The subconscious mind understands and stores only those messages which are in the form of pictures. This is because the subconscious mind can best understand the language of pictures. Before we send any message to our subconscious mind, we need to calm our conscious mind with the help of relaxation.

After we achieve the Alpha state of mind – when our subconscious mind is ready to accept our messages, we should send the messages in the form of vivid visuals with complete details.

Add animation to these pictures. The more animation we can add, the better it is. To do this, we should visualize a blank screen in our mind, just at the forehead. Then we should project on that screen a picture that shows that we have already achieved our goal. Visualize involving as many of your five senses as possible. Add as many colors, emotions and special effects as you can. Once our subconscious mind accepts these visuals, it starts working to make them a reality.

Review these images everyday with renewed vigor and emotions. To derive maximum benefits, relaxation should be done at a specific time and place for 20 minutes. Repeated daily, visualization will help us achieve our goal faster. Remember, effective visualization is the key to success.

6. Give auto-suggestions

Auto-suggestion, as the name suggests, refer to the suggestions you give to your own subconscious mind. Auto-suggestions facilitate the achievement of our goal. By giving auto-suggestions to ourselves, we can increase our confidence and ward off any negative thoughts that might undermine the achievement of our goal. In a way, they act like a shield.

For example, a student, Ms. Visualizer, who is from a middle-class family, decides upon the goal to work for NASA (National Aeronautics and Space Administration) in the USA and become a part of a space expedition.

She has a great burning desire and diligence to do so. But what will happen when Ms. Visualizer discloses her plans to her family, relatives, friends etc.? They may ridicule her by calling her a 'day dreamer' and try to dissuade her from pursuing her goal and ask her to aim for something less extraordinary. Thus, you can see how one is vulnerable to negative suggestions on the way to achieving a goal. Giving auto-suggestions to oneself is a great way to develop immunity from all such negative influences.

I urge all of you, never to accept anything less than what you have aimed for. The subconscious mind will enable you to achieve whatever you want, only if you have faith in yourself.

7. Use maximum catalysts

Catalyst is a term borrowed from Chemistry. It refers to a substance whose presence in a chemical reaction speeds up the reaction, but it does not take part in the reaction itself. In terms of programming the subconscious mind, a catalyst refers to that activity which speeds up the process of achievement of bur goal.

There are six such catalysts:

1. Fasting 　　　　2. Silence

3. Prayer 　　　　4. Positive thinking

5. Meditation 　　　6. Alpha music

7.1 Fasting

Almost all religions stress the importance of fasting. In Hinduism, there are many instances in which fasting has been linked to the achievement of goals. For example, on the day of "Karwa Chauth,' married women fast so that their husbands may live long. In Islam, Muslims fast during the month of Ramadan to strengthen their connection with Allah. Lent is a period of fasting for the Christians. Fasting is central to Jain religion. Every major religion has fasting at some time or the other as part of its observances.

Are these just arbitrary connections, or is there a scientific explanation for the link between fasting and the achievement of goals? After learning about the subconscious mind, I am convinced that this link has a scientific explanation.

It is the tendency of our body to direct more blood supply to the organ that is more active. When we eat, our stomach becomes active, and it attracts a sizeable amount of blood supply, some of which is diverted from nearby organs–like the solar plexus which, as we know, is the seat of the subconscious mind.

When we fast, the stomach does not need excessive blood supply, and the Solar plexus gets its fair share, thus strengthening the functioning of the subconscious mind. As a result, the subconscious mind becomes more active, and works more effectively towards the achievement of our goal. In this way, fasting works as a catalyst in the achievement of our goal.

7.2. Silence

Speaking is an activity that is directed by the conscious mind. When we are speaking, our conscious mind is continuously active. When we are silent, we come closer to the Alpha state of mind. In such a state, chances of communication between the subconscious mind and the conscious mind are very high.
During such communication, the subconscious mind may reveal its plan for the achievement of our goals in the form of flashes, intuitions, hunches etc. So if we observe silence as often as we can, the subconscious mind will get an opportunity to communicate with us and we will be able to catch certain significant opportunities that take us towards our goal.

We can identify the messages of our subconscious mind through regular practice of silence. We must therefore observe silence regularly for faster achievement of our goal.

7.3 Prayer

Prayer is of prime importance in every religion and is understood to be the primary channel of communicating with God. During prayer, our mind

and all our senses get relaxed and we are filled with positive emotions. Whatever we visualize during this mental state will be easily accepted by the subconscious mind.

We usually pray in silence. Silence brings a sense of inner consciousness in us. This inner consciousness activates our subconscious mind to receive cosmic power from the Higher Intelligence (God). When a group of people pray together for a specific cause, a collective consciousness is created which has been described by Napoleon Hill as the 'Master Mind Principle' in his famous book 'Law of Success.' This collective consciousness in its advanced stage leads to universal consciousness which helps in the quick achievement of the desired objective. This is why collective prayer is more effective than individual prayer.

It is very important to know the fact that a prayer is more effective when done for others than for oneself e.g., relatives or friends. And it is most effective when it is done for unknown persons. So, if we wish to increase our prayer's effectiveness and power, we should pray for the people who are not in any way related to us. For example, we can pray for the orphans whenever we pass by an orphanage, for patients whenever we pass by a hospital, for the poor whenever we pass a beggar or a tramp on the street and for humanity on the whole.

Once you get into the habit of praying for unknown persons, you will never need to pray for yourself. Even if you need to do so, your prayer will be much more powerful, In this way, prayer acts as a catalyst for our subconscious mind. Mahatma Gandhi's life evidences the power of fasting, silence and prayers in achieving lofty goals.

7.4. Positive thinking

The best way to keep negative thoughts away from our mind is to fill our mind completely with positive thoughts. Do not leave even an iota of space for any kind of negative thoughts. Always keep yourself occupiedwithpositive thoughts such as, "The world is a great place to live in.", "People love and respect me,", "Things are getting better everyday,", "I have a very bright future ahead." etc. Repetition of positive thoughts converts them into positive beliefs which manifest as positive events. It is the law of the subconscious mind that positive beliefs transform into a positive future while negative beliefs transformation into a ruined future. It is aptly said, "Whatever you believe, you shall achieve."

7.5. Meditation

When we meditate, our brain-wave frequency reduces and we experience either Alpha or Theta state of mind With constant practice of reaching Alpha state (by meditation), we can command our subconscious mind at anytime. Thus, meditation acts as a catalyst to reach the Alpha state of mind.

7.6. Alpha music

Music is of two types-the type of music that increases your brain activity and the type of music that decreases it. The music that decreases our brain activity is known as Alpha music. Listening to Alpha music reduces our brain wave frequency and helps us achieve the Alpha state of mind. Studying while such pleasant Alpha music is being played in the background helps us in concentrating and memorizing our lessons easily. We have produced Alpha music CD to help everyone for this purpose. It is available from the addresses given on the last page of this book.

8. Wait patiently for the result

The Bhagvad Gita, one of the holy books of Hindus, teaches us that nobody can get anything before its proper time and more than what that peson actually deserves. It teaches us to wait patiently for the results. If we reframe the same saying in the concept of mind power, it could be read as, "Nobody can achieve anything before the proper time and more than what he has visualized." Thus, when we know that we can get our goal only when it is the right time, why not relax and wait patiently for it to get transformed into a physical reality? Always trust the powers of your subconscious mind. If you doubt them, you will damage the image of your goal in the memory bank of your subconscious mind and in turn damage your own future.

What do you do after you have ploughed the field, sown the seeds, added the fertilizers, and nourished it with water everyday? Do you doubt the growing of your plants? Do you check its progress by taking out the seeds again and again? Of course not. By doing that you are actually reducing the chances of the seeds' growth and that of its transformation into a plant. Similarly, once you have set your goal, the only thing you can do is to visualize it daily with intense faith. At the proper time, your goal will automatically transform into reality. This is the law of nature.

Steps to achieve success in life

Study this diagram. The upper half of it shows working of conscious mind and the lower half shows working of subconscious mind. The journey of our success starts from setting our goal and ends on achieving our goal.

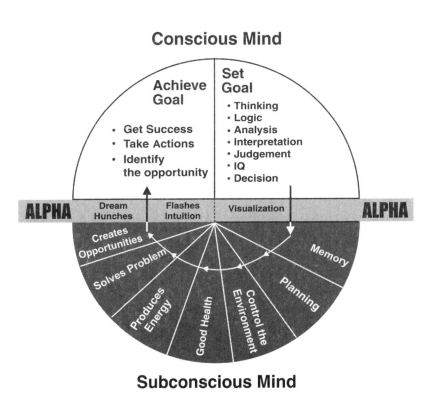

Following are the steps to achieve success:

1. **Set your goal** with the help of your conscious mind. You may need to use some of the powers of your conscious mind such as thinking, logic, analysis, interpretation and judgment before you decide on a goal.

2. Communicate your goal to the subconscious mind by visualizing it in Alpha state of mind.

3. The subconscious mind stores the pictures of your goal in its memory.

4. Now your subconscious mind will start planning for the achievement of your goal.

5. The subconscious mind creates an environment and opportunities favorable to your goal.

6. Subconscious mind will solve your problems if they arise.

7. Once the subconscious mind has done planning, solved problems and created favorable environment and opportunities it will start giving you signals through dream, hunches, flashes or intuition.

8. Identify and seize the opportunities with the help of your conscious mind.

9. Take action with the help of your conscious mind.

10. Achieve the goal through the co-ordination of your conscious and subconscious mind.

Working of the conscious and subconscious mind depends upon the clarity of your visualization and ability to go into the Alpha state of mind.

Prerequisites for programming

(Operating system)—— Burning desire

We are familiar with the crucial role of operating system in any computer. It is a prerequisite for running any program on the computer. In same way, there is a prerequisite for running any program in the  subconscious mind. This operating system is your burning desire to achieve your goal. In his world-famous book. Think and Grow Rich, Napoleon Hill has allotted the first chapter to explaining the need for a burning desire in the accomplishment of a goal.

Burning desire means an intense desire and total dedication to succeed. Before you can achieve any desired goal, you need to prepare yourself. Recall the devotion of Meerabai towards Lord Krishna! She had such a burning desire to meet Him that she chose to drink poison rather than give up her devotion for him.

(Electric supply)—— Faith

Just as a computer need constant supply of electricity without any interruption, so does our subconscious mind need a constant supply of faith. This is the faith in the ability of the subconscious mind to achieve your goal. To get the best result of your program, you must have full faith in your subconscious mind.

(Computer virus)—— Doubt

A computer virus disrupts the working of a computer. At times, it can corrupt an entire hard disk. Similarly, the subconscious mind can get afflicted by a virus of doubt. These doubts act as viruses and even destroy all programs fed to the subconscious mind.

Recall the story of Ramayana (a Hindu epic) in which Hanuman and his fellow monkeys construct a bridge of stones. The stones floated because of the monkeys' faith that they would do so. When Lord Rama heard about this, he had doubts. He tried to float a stone using the same technique, but his stone sunk. The power of faith that worked for the monkeys did not work in his case. If you do not want your program to fail, be careful and have no doubts.

The most important prerequisites for programming:
1. Give unconditional forgiveness
2. Give unconditional love

Nature has provided us with a wonderful computer in the form of our subconscious mind, which if used properly can give us excellent results. But we keep it busy with negative emotions such as jealousy, hatred, anger, frustration, etc. If we want to make the best use of our subconscious mind, we need to free ourselves from all kinds of negative emotions that take up most of our time and energy. To do this, we need to learn to forgive ourselves and others. I believe what Louise Hay says: "Every disease is the result of state of un-forgiveness." So forgive everyone concerned and you will feel so light as if you have been relieved of a heavy burden.

It is not necessary to talk about or communicate our intent to forgive to the person concerned. We just need to forgive them in our own mind. There is a simple process to do this. When you are relaxed, preferably in the Alpha state, visualize the face of the person you are angry with or the one who has hurt you. Then recite this sentence repeatedly till the face of the person disappears on its own – "I unconditionally forgive you for your behavior and pray to God to give you health, wealth and happiness."

How would you know whether you have really forgiven your enemy? When you meet or think of that person, if you become tense and angry, it means you still haven't forgiven him. If a natural smile comes to your face, it means you have indeed forgiven him. Once you fulfill the precondition of total forgiveness, the stage for unconditional love automatically sets in. These are the preconditions for programming.

Caution

While using your subconscious mind, keep in mind these simple precautions:

1. It is important to understand that we do not need to give any specific directions to the subconscious mind regarding the achievement of our goal. Doing so indicates that we do not have full faith in its abilities and as a result it stops working for the achievement of our goal.

2. We also need not force our subconscious mind in any way. After giving orders to it, we just need to relax and wait. It is a very faithful servant that works according to our orders but resents any type of pressure. Putting pressure on the subconscious mind indicates our lack of trust in its abilities.

From what age can programming be done

Before conception

Programming the subconscious mind of a child can be done even before conception by its would be parents. If the father and mother sit together and visualize the child they desire (son or daughter), they will surely get the one they visualize.

During pregnancy

Programming by the parents is also possible during pregnancy. The episode of Abhimanyu is very well narrated in Mahabharata. Napoleon Hill, in his famous book Think and Grow Rich, states that he started the programming of the subconscious mind of his son from the time his wife was pregnant. The doctors, using ultrasound had diagnosed that the child would be born without ears and hence would be deaf throughout his life. Napoleon Hill, instead of getting discouraged by the diagnosis, took it as a challenge. His suggestions had a deep impact on the subconscious mind of his son who started leading a normal life in spite of the absence of

ears. Eventually, he regained his normal hearing and even graduated from a regular University.

In the cradle

A little child can also be effectively programmed even when it is still in the cradle. We can find many such cases in history. In India, Chhatrapati Shivaji Maharaj, the great Maratha king, is the best example of such a programming.

His mother Jijabai used to sing songs full of patriotism and bravery. This subconscious programming by his mother during childhood helped him to scale great heights as a king who defended his motherland.

During school days

When a child is in the school, he is programmed by his teachers. In fact, teachers are the most effective programmers because children trust them implicitly.

Any time during the life

After a child becomes an adult, it can learn to program its mind on its own. Children should be taught the technique of self programming, so that they can shape their own future with faith and confidence. Everyone has the right to be the 'master of his fate and the captain of his soul'.

Learn practically how to use the powers of your subconscious mind

On continuous demand from readers of this book and participants of my seminars I have started an unique practical training program for those who are interested to learn from me how to use the power of subconscious mind practically. This one day workshop is conducted in all major cities of India, Africa, Europe, Far East and USA.

This practical program is a training for your conscious mind of how to use subconscious mind. In this workshop I train participants how to reprogram their minds positively. Participants are taken to alpha state frequently under my guidence and their goals are installed while they are in that state. I also teach

103

them some advance techniques to use the power of subconscious mind such as Problem Solving, Spiritual Healing, Removing Phobia, Changing Beliefs etc.

This workshop is very usefull to businessmen, proffesionals, housewives, students, creative people and for all, for betterment of their life.

The person desirous to attend this
'Adhia Mind Power Workshop'
should contact our corporate office,
Adhia Academy,
between 10 am to 6 pm (I.S.T.)
on +91-79-2675 44 99, 6521 79 23
during all the working days
or visit my website
www.adhiammindpower.com
or send email on
jeetadhia@yahoo.co.in
or info@adhiamindpower.com

Reprogramming of our mind renovates our life.

Can our program fail

YES, the subconscious mind, under certain specific circumstances, cannot produce the desired results of programming. The reasons are summarized below.

☞ When we do not trust the power of the subconscious mind, it does not give us the desired results.

☞ When we constantly use negative sentences in our daily conversation, we may not get the desired results even though our goal is positive.

☞ When we become impatient for the achievement of our goal, after handing it over to the subconscious mind. In short, it signals that we do not trust our subconscious mind. How can it work without your trust?

☞ When we try to give directions to our subconscious mind about the method of working towards our goal. This disrupts and may even go against the plan it has already made for achieving our goal.

☞ When we are unable to control the constant flow of negative emotions to our mind. When our mind is filled with negative emotions, a thunder and lightning storm is triggered in our brain which distorts the mental images of our goal. These images are needed for continuous reference by the subconscious mind in the process of planning. Thus, in the presence of negative emotions, our subconscious mind is not able to materialize our goal into a reality.

How the subconscious mind communicates with us

Our subconscious mind communicates with our conscious mind in the following ways:

- Intuitions
- Hunches
- Dreams
- Flashes

Our conscious and subconscious minds communicate on a regular basis. This communication is essential for the execution of the plan our subconscious mind has made for the achievement of our goal. You might recall, the subconscious mind understands the language of images only.

Therefore, the conscious mind communicates with the subconscious mind with the help of images, while the subconscious mind communicates with the conscious mind in many different ways. It usually does this when the conscious mind is fully or partially inactive. That is why I emphasize the importance of silence as a catalyst in programming. The main channels of communication for the subconscious mind in communicating with the conscious mind are intuitions, hunches, dreams and flashes.

If we want divine guidance from our subconscious mind, it is essential for us to learn to interpret the language of the subconscious mind and also the method of accessing its messages. The discovery of Insulin in a dream by Dr. Fredrick Banting, which at first seems accidental, was actually a revelation by the subconscious mind.

Have you had an experience where in all your conscious attempts to find a solution to a problem had been unsuccessful, but when you relaxed your mind and freed it of all thoughts, a solution suddenly occurred to you? Actually what you experienced was a communication from the subconscious mind in the form of a flash.

Suppose it is your goal to be healthy and you are living an inactive life and one fine morning you feel like going for a brisk walk, it is an intuition. If you suddenly feel keen on doing something you had decided about long back, it means the subconscious mind has communicated with you through a hunch or a flash.

How to get directions from the subconscious mind

Whenever we face a problem and we are unable to find a solution, instead of getting tense and frustrated, we should approach our subconscious mind. The subconscious mind is a treasure house of knowledge and wisdom and has a solution to every problem.

In addition, it is completely trustworthy and is eager to serve us. Thus, it is very desirable for us to approach the subconscious mind every time we have a problem which we feel cannot be solved by our conscious mind.

If you have a particular problem or a decision to make, collect all the related facts and options and go to sleep while thinking about them. Just before falling asleep, tell your subconscious mind, "This is a problem I cannot solve with my conscious powers. So I pass this problem to you." After having done this, sleep peacefully because your trustworthy servant is already set to work. It will reveal its plan to you through a dream, flash, intuition or hunch.

Factors influencing the subconscious mind

There are some factors which can influence the subconscious mind either in a positive or a negative way.

Thoughts

The conscious mind is the source of all thoughts – both negative and positive. Positive thoughts nourish the subconscious mind whereas negative thoughts are detrimental to healthy growth of the mind and body. Even though we have a high goal which we visualize religiously everyday but if we fail to control the inflow of negative thoughts, they will hinder the achievement of our goal. So positive thinking is essential for success.

Belief

A thought or an idea which is accepted as truth is known as a belief. If we really want to progress in life, we need to analyze the origin and evolution of our beliefs. It does not matter whether the belief is right or wrong but what matter is whether it is an empowering or disempowering belief. By analyzing we can distinguish a disempowering belief from an empowering one and can change our disempowering beliefs into empowering ones. Once we do this, our approach to life will become more and more positive.

As a result, our subconscious mind will become more empowered to give us positive results.

Emotions

Just as thoughts can be classified into positive and negative, emotions too can  be classified as positive and negative. Negative emotions are very harmful. They reduce the potential of our mind. Therefore, always be careful to allow only positive emotions such as love, compassion, forgiveness, mercy and faith to enter and be a constant part of your life.

Spoken words

The subconscious mind is influenced to a great extent by the words we or other people speak our daily life.

Our spoken words possess the power to change our lives.  For example, a couple wants their child to be happy and successful in life but they do not understand the effect of spoken words on their child. Hence they use negative statements like "You are completely dumb.", "You can't do anything in your life.", etc. These sentences affect the subconscious mind of the child. When these sentences are accepted by the subconscious mind of the child, they ruin his future. If you really want your child to be happy and successful, don't give any negative suggestions. Instead, keep on nourishing his or her mind with encouraging words like "We love you very much.", "You are a good son or daughter.", "We are glad to have you as our child", "You will be very successful in life" etc. Use these magical sentences and see how your child scales the height of success.

Behavior

Once we decide a specific goal, we must start behaving in accordance with it. By doing this, we send strong messages to our subconscious mind for working towards our goal. For instance, a person's goal is to become a respectable member of the society. But if the behavior is disrespectful towards others, s/he will not be successful in achieving that goal. What s/he needs to do is to match the visualization with appropriate behavior. Soon that goal will be transformed into reality.

Visualization

By now, you are clear that the subconscious mind understands the language of images mainly. So our greatest tool in achieving success is visualization. Create appropriate images that depict your goal and see the same pictures on your mental screen. In this way, the pictures get imprinted in your memory bank and used by the subconscious mind in the planning process. Thus, if your goal is to be a successful business person, every day visualize yourself getting the Businessman of the Year Award with vivid details till you achieve the goal. Parents should encourage their children to use this technique to achieve desired and positive objectives.

Hope

Hope is like a nourishing tonic for the subconscious mind. On the other hand, hopelessness reduces the potential of the subconscious mind. If you continue nourishing your subconscious mind with hopeful or optimistic thoughts, you can be sure of achieving success. What every you expect will happen.

Faith

As I have mentioned earlier, our inner computer, the subconscious mind needs a constant uninterrupted supply of electrical current called faith. The working of our subconscious mind gets disturbed if there are voltage fluctuations in its supply. So be sure to supply your mind with a continuous and smooth flow of faith to achieve your goal.

Doubts

When the virus in the form of doubts enters our mind, it completely destroys the programs stored in its hard disk.

Therefore, never allow this virus to enter your mind and also shield your family members from being infected.

Never doubt the potential of the subconscious mind. I have seen many instances of parents who doubt the potential of their own children as effective managers of their life, even when these children are grown up, happily married and financially secure. Never do this to your children. It indicates that you doubt the power of the subconscious mind of your child. If this virus enters the hard disk of your child, it will sabotage its chances of success. So, beware of and keep away from the virus of doubt.

Burning desire

There is a story of a man who approached a sage to know the 'purpose of life'. The sage asked him to follow him while he crossed a river. The man did so, and while they were in the middle of the river, the sage caught hold of the man's head and submerged it under water. He held it there for a while, not allowing him to escape. When he finally managed  to bring his head above water, the sage asked him: "What was your greatest desire when your head was underwater?" The gasping man replied: "I had a strong desire to breathe air." The sage then replied, "When you desire to know the 'purpose of life' as badly as you desired air while under the water, come back to me, I promise to tell you the purpose of life at that time." You too must have a burning desire of this intensity to achieve your goal.

Joke

Always remember that the subconscious mind does not understand a joke. This fact is repeatedly emphasized because people tend to commit the same mistake again and again. Always be careful that our jokes do not convey any kind of negative message to our subconscious mind or to that of anyone else.

Take care of the factors that affect your subconscious mind and you will surely find success and happiness in life. Remember the cosmic law: 'what you expect happens."

Success or happiness

Till now we have talked about achieving success. But what is more important in our life – success or happiness? Would we be happy if we are only successful? It is not so. Even the most successful person on earth can be unhappy, sad and dejected. Happiness is actually a state of mind achieved by creating harmony between the physical, mental, social and spiritual aspects of life. Let us understand the way in which we can achieve this happiness.

Refer to the figure [on the next page]. In this figure the four aspects of life (physical, mental, social and spiritual) are shown as four pillars of a house. It indicates the importance of each of them in achieving happiness. Further, notice that the pillars are subdivided into parts. Each part symbolizes the aspect that needs to be attended to, in order to strengthen that pillar. If any of the four pillars are shaky, we will not be able to achieve perfect balance in life, and true happiness will always evade us. Let us discuss each of these pillars in detail

Four pillars of life

Physical

This pillar symbolizes our physical needs such as food, water, air, clothes, house etc. These are the basic needs of our life. Above all, we require good health to enjoy life.

Life Mansion

Physical (to live)	Mental (to learn)	Social (to love)	Spiritual (to contribute)
Health	Knowledge of Life	To love people	To know yourself
Career			
Wealth	Professional knowledge	To be loved by people	Contribution to society

Neglegation of any pillar
will make our life's journey very miserable

Mental

Every individual aspires to gratify his curiosity about the world and gain a wide variety of skills. This acts as an inspiration for progress. Also, specialized knowledge is essential for success in any profession. Therefore, adequate knowledge in the field of our chosen profession is important for job satisfaction and happiness.

Social

Human beings are social animals. They need constant love and support of other humans. In the absence of this love and support, their lives can become really miserable. At the same time, a person has to learn to love people, as it is the greatest force that has kept the human race alive and happy.

Spiritual

This part of life consists of two aspects. First, we need to explore the inner depths of one's own self, and second, we need to make some contribution to society. Only when we know well, our own self i.e., our principles, ethics, mission, purpose of life, etc. and are able to contribute to society, we feel real happy.

Remember, we can experience real happiness and contentment in life only when we are able to strengthen and balance these four pillars.

Books recommended For further reference

Power of Subconscious Mind *Joseph Murphy*

Your Key to Happiness *Harold Sherman*

You Can Heal Your Life *Louise Hay*

Law Of Success *Napoleon Hill*

Think and Grow Rich *Napoleon Hill*

Unilimited Power *Anthony Robins*

Awaken the Giant Within *Anthony Robins*

Creating Affluence *Deepak Chopra*

Seven Spiritual Laws of Success *Deepak Chopra*

Ageless Body, Timeless Mind *Deepak Chopra*

Creative Visualization *Denning and Philips*

Positive Imaging *Norman Vincent Peale*

You will see it, when you believe it *Wayne Dyer*

Game of Life and How to Play it *Florence Schinn*

Silva Mind Control Method *Jose Suva*

The Other 90% *Robert K. Cooper*

Love, Medicine & Miracle *Bernie Siegei*

Living with Himalayan Masters *Swami Rama*

Autobiography of a Yogi *Paramahansa Yogananda*

Mind Power *Christian H. Godefroy*

Places of seminars and workshops

BUSINESS HOUSES & CORPORATES

- Birla Cellulosic
- Reliance Infocom
- Raymond Denim
- Raymond Woolen
- Indian Rayon
- Rand Water (South Africa)
- Mafatlal Group
- Suzlon Energy Ltd.
- Gujarat State Fertilizer Corporation
- Hotel Holiday Inn (USA)
- KRIBHCO
- Paramount Industries
- J.B. Diamond
- D. Navinchandra & Co.
- K. Girdhar
- Zadafia Brothers
- Shri Harikrishna Export
- Shri Ramkrishna Export
- Munjani Brothers
- Bhargovi Gems
- Godhani Gems
- Bhavani Gems
- Manhattan Jewellery (China)
- J.B. Jewelleries (Hongkong)
- Miral Gems (Bangkok)
- Davaria Brothers
- Sahajanand Technology
- Bharat Sanchar Nigam Limited
- Punjab National Bank
- Amway
- RMP
- Swadeshi
- Modicare
- LIC of India
- Grand Polycoat
- Mehsana Steel
- Torrent - Ahmedabad Electricity Corporation
- Rajkot Nagarik Sahakari Bank Ltd.
- Varracha Co.op Bank Ltd.

GOVERNMENT/ SEMI GOVERNMENT ORGANIZATIONS

- Gujarat State Judicial Academy
- Gujarat State Financial Services Ltd.
- Gujarat Safai Kamdar Vikas Nigam
- Gujarat Maritime Board
- Gujarat Electricity Board
- Collector's Office - Surat
- D.D.O. Office - Dang
- Valsad Nagar Palika
- Agriculture Department Govt. of Guj.
- Dist. Education and Training Center
- Gujarat State Prohibition Department
- Jilla Rojgar Vinimay Kacheri
- Reserve Bank of India

Religious/Spiritual Organizations

- Akshar Purshottam Swaminarayan Temple (India, Africa, U.K., U.S.A.)
- Brahmakumaris (India, U.K., U.S.A.)
- Gayatri Parivar
- Jain Upashray
- Vaishnav Haveli
- Shivanand Ashram
- Prempuri Ashram
- Jalaram Mandir
- Shri Haridham - Sokhda
- Theosofical Society of India

- Prayosha Sansthan
- Sanatan Dharma Temple (Los Angeles)

EDUCATIONAL ORGANIZATIONS

- Gujarat University
- Nirma University
- Gujarat Vidhyapith
- Dr. Babasaheb Ambedkar Open University
- Riverside Community College (California)
- New Sharda Mandir School (South Africa)
- Delhi Public School
- Shri Swaminarayan Gurukul
- L.D. Engineering College
- J.N.T.U. College of Engineering - Hydrabad
- Lokbharti - Sanosara
- Omkar English Medium School
- Pharmacy College - Anand
- Medical College - Yavatmal
- College of Nursing - Ahmedabad

SOCIAL ORGANIZATION

- Rotary Club
- Rotaract Club
- Jaycee's Club
- Lions Club
- Leo Club
- Jain Social Group
- Jain Jagruti Center
- Inner Wheel Club
- Laughing Club
- Yuvak Biradari
- Bharat Vikas Parishad
- Halai Lohana Mahajan
- Patel Social Group
- Mahavir Social Group
- Sardar Patel Trust
- Manthan Foundation
- Senior Citizen Forum
- Agrawal Samaj

- Retired Officer's Forum
- Shri Gujarati Pragati Samaj - Hydrabad
- NSS
- 'Life' (Rajkot)
- Hindu Society of North Carilina
- Gujarat Cultural Society (Dallas)
- All India Students Association
- Ahmedabad Menopause Club

PROFESSIONAL ORGANIZATIONS

- Indian Engineering Association
- Indian Medical Association
- Indian Dental Association of California
- The Insitute of Chartered Accountants of India
- Association of cost accountants of India
- Ahmedabad Building Contractors Association
- Indian Small Scale Paint Association
- Assocation of LIC Agents
- Asian American Hotel Owners Association
- Institute of Engineers
- Indian Revenue Service Association
- RBI Staff Consumers Co.Op. Society
- Bharuch Management Association
- Shramjivi Parishad
- Sahakar Bharti
- Bhavnagar District Small Industries Association
- Drugist & Chemist Association
- Gandhinagar Electronic Zone Industries Association
- Income Tax Employees Federation
- GIDC - Mehsana

Requirements for
seminar / workshop on this subject

1. An auditorium to the capacity of the audience. (Preferably air-conditioned)
2. Three phase electric supply with earthing.
3. Minimum 200 participants.
3. Good quality sound system.
4. Seminar will require minimum five hours. Workshop will require two days.
5. Invitation letter soon after the confirmation of a date of seminar / workshop.
6. A "Letter of acknowledgement' as a proof of completion of the seminar / workshop.
7. Seminar/workshop can be arranged in Hindi/ English or Gujarati.
8. Facility to be provided outside the auditorium for display/sale of books/ cassettes/ CDs etc.
9. No mobile phones will be allowed in the program.
10. Advertisement should be released only after the approval of Adhia Academy.
11. If lunch is to be given during the program it should be simple working lunch.
12. No seat number will be allotted on the entry passes.
13. Advertisement posters and entry passes will be supplied by Adhia Academy at reasonable extra cost.
14. Children below 13 years are not allowed in the program.
15. The organizer need not introduce Dr. Adhia as his introduction is an integral part of his program.

Dr. Adhia's Products

Contact for Products

e-mail : rudrapublication1@gmail.com

www.rudrapublication.com **Buy online** www.clickabooks.com

For Home Delivery : Mobile : +91-99241 43847

Products Outlets

Available at **A.H. WHEELERS** Book stall
at all Railway Stations of India and S.T. Stands of Gujarat
All Gujarat CROSSWORD Branch

AHMEDABAD - 079

Rudra Book Shop : 25-B, Govt.Co-op. Soc., Navrangpura, M : 98259 25947

Mind Training Institute : 404/B, Legacy, Panjarapol Cross Road 26302660/61
R.R. Sheth & Co. : Khanpur, Tel.: 2550 6573, 2550 1732
Ajay Publication : Aaradhna Comm. Centre, Relief Road, M. 98251 50562
Rupali Book Centre : K.B. Comm. Complex, Khanpur, Tel.: 2550 44 43
Hitesh Gandhi : Nr. Thakorbhai Desai Hall, Law Garden, Tel.: 26638773
S.T. Book Stall 1 & 4 : Gita Mandir S.T. Stand, M. : 98249 75562
Gujarat Pustakalaya : 11, Ellora Comm. Centre, 2550 6973, M. 98984 67262
Uzma Publication : 12, Faiz Complex, Khanpur, Tel.: 25500790
Mosinbhai : Aastodiya, Tel.: 25350794
Vijaybhai Dobariya : Gurukul, Memnagar, Ahmedabd 098256 86900
New Prakash Book Depo : Gokul Complex, Ellisbrdige, 079-26422111
Saurashtra Staionary : Bipin Patel 9824253141 Bapunagar

ANAND - 02692 and VALLABHVIDYANAGAR

Chandan General Stores : Station Road, Anand Tel. 2660 60 99250 99590
Ambica Book Store, Nana Bazar, V.V. Nagar M 9825545261
Pustak Mahal, Nana Bazar, V.V. Nagar 9924812095, 9409012868
Pandya & Sons, Mota Bazar, V.V. Nagar 9974598026
A. H. Wheeler & Co. Pvt. Ltd. Book Stall Railway Station, 9737765438
Ajay Book Stall, "Krishna Kunj", Nr. Mota Bazar, Vidhayanagar, 99254413936

ankleshwar A. H. Wheeler (Ankleshwar) C/o. Railway Book Store 9428685597
BARDOLI - 02622
Ramesh Traders : Sardar Baug, Opp. College, Tel.: 22 78 84

BARODA - 0265

Gujrat Pustakalay Sahakari Mandali
Popular Book Centre : O/s. Yuvraj Hotel, Nr. S.T. Stand, Tel.: 279 44 24
The Allies Stores, Opp. Jubilee Gardern, Baroda, 9537648491
Sagar Book Publishers, 101-102-104, "Sukhdham Compex",
Mira Datar's Tekro, Navabazar, Baroda. 9979322746, 9879402375
Acharya Book Depot, Opp. Gandhi Nagar Gruh, Baroda. 9824286729
GangaSagar Pustakalay, Jagdish Lojni Bajuma, 9067115757, 8530151920
Maneesh Book Shop, 7, Payal Complex, Opp. M.S. University, 9898522447
Shreenath Newspaper Agency, Raopura, Baroda-390001 9898240228

Bharuch - 02642
A. H. Wheeler Railway Station, Bharuch 9723268037
Prajapati Book Store, 9879237236, 9898214517, 9898368426
Harilal Maganlal & Co., Katopore Gate, Bharuch - 392001 9227135356
Thakkar Book Depot, M. 9228299695, 9228176199
BHAVNAGAR - 0278
Kitab Ghar : High Court Road, Tel.: 5213257 M.: 98983 97271
Prasar : Rupani-Atabhai Road, **Lok Milap** : 1565, Sardar Nagar, Tel.: 256 64 02,
S.T. Stand Book Stall : S.T. Stand
BHUJ - 02832 **Sahajanand Rural Trust** : *G.M.D.C. Guest House, M.: 9825227509*

Bilimora-2634 Arjunsinh Engineer : M. : 9998045188
GANDHINAGAR-02712
Hariom Stationery : BG Dist. Shopping Centre, Sector-21, M.: 99244 55882
HIMMATNAGAR-02772 Pravinsinh Zala : (M) +91-91734 18280
JAMNAGAR - 0288
School Point : Nr. St. Xaviers High School, M.: 98980 71514
Kirit Bhatt : Manu Farsan : Bardhan Chowk, Tel.: 2675512, 9898574748
JETPUR - 02823 Vidya Book Store : Opp. Central Bank Tel.: 221516
JUNAGADH - 0285
Kesari News Agency : Kalva Chowk, Tel.: 265 09 43, 265 48 19
Prerna Nu Jharnu Sahitya Book Stores : Mira Complex, M.: 98242 11446
LIMDI - 2752
Darshan Hotel : National Highway,
Jamuna Hotel : Nr. Jamuna Hotel, National Highway M.: 98248 13804
MEHSANA - 02762
Dinesh Prajapati: 44, Aashadipa Soc., Opp. Nirma Factory, M.: 94260 86244
Gujarat Pustakalaya : 1, Sardar Shoping Centre, Tel.: 252 426
Piyush Pustak Bhandar : Nr. S.T. Stand, 220350, (M) 98258 88 778
NADIAD-0268
Mohmadbhai, S.T. Bus Stand, Nadiad 9974336344
Honey Book Centre, Old Bus Depot, Nadiad 9277951521
A. H. Wheeler & Co. Pvt. Ltd. Book Stall Railway Station, 9737765438
Student Book Stall, 13-14, Chankya Complex, Nadiad 9825438399
NAVSARI-02637
Mansukhlal & Sons, Dudhiya Talav Road, Navsari 9428163480
College Store, Topiwala Mansion, Opp. Garda College, 9825099121
New College Road, 1, Dadabhai Navroji Shoping Centre, 9898215999
Shah Chatrabhuj Nanchand, Mota Bazar, Navsari 9879199651, 9727840900
PALANPUR - 02742
Treasure : Jivan Jyot Bldg, Jahanara Baug Road, Tel.: 225 13 20
Killol Enterprise : 106, White House, Tel.: 25 56 96 M.: 94263 88053
PATAN - 2766 Modern Book Stall : Opp. Bus Stand, Tel.: (O) 220129 (R) 22 10 09
PORBANDAR - 0286 Jayendra Chotai : Manish Stores, M. 99790 11011
RAJKOT - 0281
Johar Cards : 'Hasnain' Dr.Yagnik Road, Tel.: 246 22 52, M : 98242 10492
Pravin Pustak Bhandar : Opp. Rajkot Mun.Corp., Tel.:232460, 234602
Rajesh Book Shop : Yagnik Road, M.: 99241 33519
Bharat Book Store: Yagnik Road, Tel.:2465148
Ravi Prakashan : Yagnik Road, Tel.: 246 06 25, 248 34 90
Old & New Book Stall : Yagnik Road,
Rajesh Book Stall : Opp. Lodhawad Police Chowkv, Tel.: 2233518
Minerwa Footware : Dharmendra Road, M.: 9898119097
Sanjeevani Ayurvedic Store : 2, Siddhnath Complex opp. Jivan jyot
School,University Road Rajkot: Ph:9879878328,02812583755
SURAT-0261
Indira Book Stall, Nr. Jain Dharmshala, Opp. Railway Station, 9879193114
Gajanan Pustkalay : Opp Commerce House, Tel. : 242 42 46, M : 98244 83772
Gajanan Book Depot : Tower Road, Tel. : 2365 49 21 M : 98797 40059
Panvala Stores : Lal Gate, Musha Chasmavalani Gali, Tel. : 243 71 55
Surat Book Centre : 9/48, Kotsafil Road, Opp. Dena Bank
Tel.:243 69 11 M.: 98790 44220